December 1st 1838

My Dear companion I take
this oppertunity to inform you
that we arrived in Liberty and
committed to Jool this evening
but we are all in good spirits
Captain bogard will hand you
this line my respects to all
remain where you are at preasant
yours &C ———— Joseph Smith Jr

LOVE LETTERS
of *Joseph* and *Emma*

*To my wonderful husband
whose anxious concern for his wife reminds me a great deal
of Joseph's solicitous ministrations to Emma* —A.E.

To my devoted husband —L.L.S.

ACKNOWLEDGMENTS

I want to thank Desirée Johns, my infinitely amazing and talented editorial, research, and writing assistant. Her insights and skills were more than invaluable, and her passion for the subject resulted in wonderful finds that literally made this book.

I would also like to thank everyone in Covenant's editorial, design, and marketing departments—so many people contributed, and I don't want to leave anyone out; Covenant boasts some of the hardest-working and most talented people I know, and I'm infinitely grateful to have them as my team on this project. I also want to thank Jessica Warner for rendering her incredible design talents on behalf of this work. Lastly, I am appreciative that artists like Liz Lemon Swindle grace us with the fruits of their imagination—her work always prompts me to ponder the depths of emotion the Prophet felt for his beloved Emma and his Savior.

Note to the Reader:

A number of unpublished sources are quoted in this book.
Spelling, punctuation, capitalization, and grammar have been standardized where necessary to improve readability.

All sketches and paintings © Liz Lemon Swindle. Courtesy of Foundation Arts. For print information, visit www.foundationarts.com.
Letter images courtesy of the Church Archives, The Church of Jesus Christ of Latter-day Saints.

Jacket and book design by Jessica A. Warner, © 2008 Covenant Communications, Inc.

Published by Covenant Communications, Inc.
American Fork, Utah

Printed in Canada
First Printing: October 2008

15 14 13 12 11 10 09 08   10 9 8 7 6 5 4 3 2 1

ISBN-13 978-1-59811-718-9
ISBN-10 1-59811-718-1

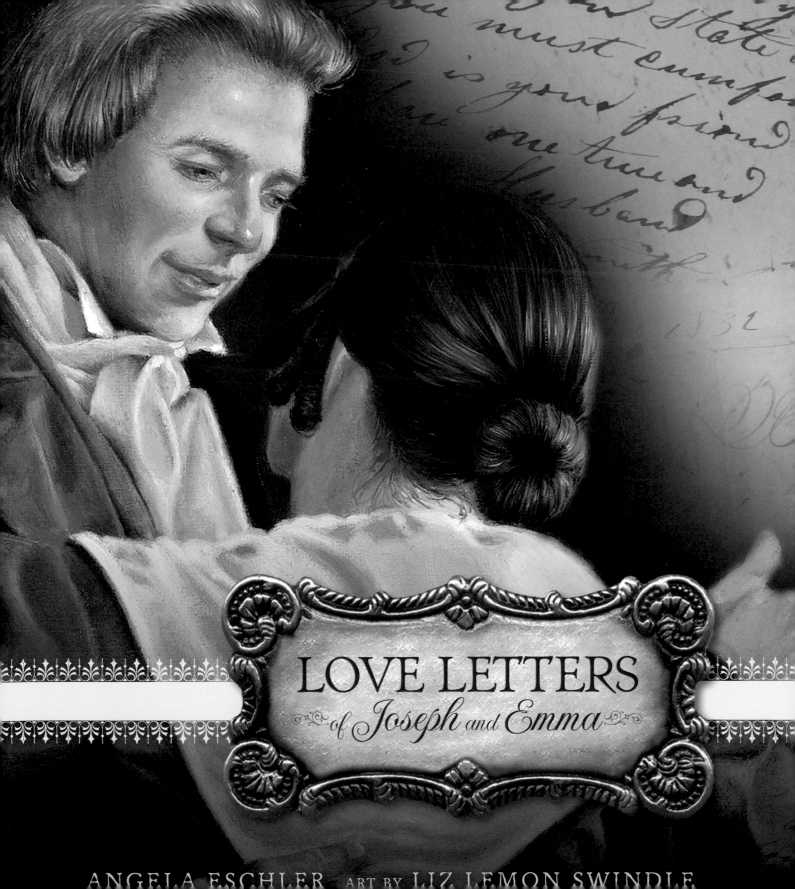

LOVE LETTERS
of Joseph and Emma

ANGELA ESCHLER   ART BY LIZ LEMON SWINDLE

LOVE and DEVOTION

Let thy soul delight in thy husband . . .

—Revelation to Emma, Doctrine & Covenants 25:14

That thy faithfulness is stronger than the cords of death.

—Revelation to Joseph, Doctrine & Covenants 121:44

In 1825, Joseph was working in Harmony, Pennsylvania, when he first met a tall, dark-haired schoolteacher with a quick wit and lively sense of humor. For a young man whose life was filled with such unusual solemnity, what joy her acquaintance must have been. Later describing her as "the choice of [his] heart,"[1] Joseph importuned Emma Hale to be his bride.

Theirs was not to be a fêted union. Because of her father's strong disapproval of Joseph—a man who claimed to have seen visions and whose financial prospects were dim—Joseph and Emma were forced to elope, celebrating a secret wedding on January 18, 1827, in South Bainbridge, New York. He was only twenty-one years old, she but twenty-two.

As Emma related later, Joseph convinced her to participate in the clandestine operation on the spur of the moment. She simply set off one day to visit the Stowell home, having "no intention of marrying when I left." However, after being cajoled by Joseph while there, and since—she noted good-humoredly—she preferred "to marry him more than anyone [else she] knew," she "consented."[2]

Their marriage lasted only seventeen brief years, cut short by the ruthless bullets of a mob that resulted in the heartbreaking martyrdom of a devoted husband. But theirs was the assurance of an everlasting reunion on the other side of the veil: shortly after 5 PM on May 28, 1843, Hyrum Smith officiated in "The Old Homestead" as Joseph and Emma were sealed for time and all eternity.

1. *History of the Church* 5:107.
2. Emma to her sons, Joseph III and Alexander, February 1879 (Document titled: Emma Hale Smith Bidamon, "Emma Smith's Last Testimony," Community of Christ Archives.)

LETTER FROM JOSEPH TO EMMA

WRITTEN IN LIBERTY JAIL, MISSOURI ❦ 4 APRIL 1839

If you want to know how much I want to see you, examine your feelings, how much you want to see me, and judge for yourself. I would gladly walk from here to you barefoot and bareheaded and half naked to see you and think it great pleasure, and never count it toil. . . .

LETTER FROM JOSEPH TO EMMA

WRITTEN IN RICHMOND, MISSOURI ❦ 12 NOVEMBER 1838

O, my affectionate Emma. I want you to remember that I am a true and faithful friend, to you and all the children, forever. My heart is entwined around yours forever and ever. Oh, may God bless you all. Amen.

EMMA'S BLESSING

WRITTEN IN NAUVOO, ILLINOIS ❧ 1844

A blessing Emma wrote for herself, having asked Joseph
for a blessing right before he left for Carthage. Not having time, he told her to write the best blessing
she could, and he would sign it upon his return. He never returned.

I desire with all my heart to honor and respect my

husband . . . ever to live in his confidence and by

acting in unison with him, retain the place which

God has given me by his side.

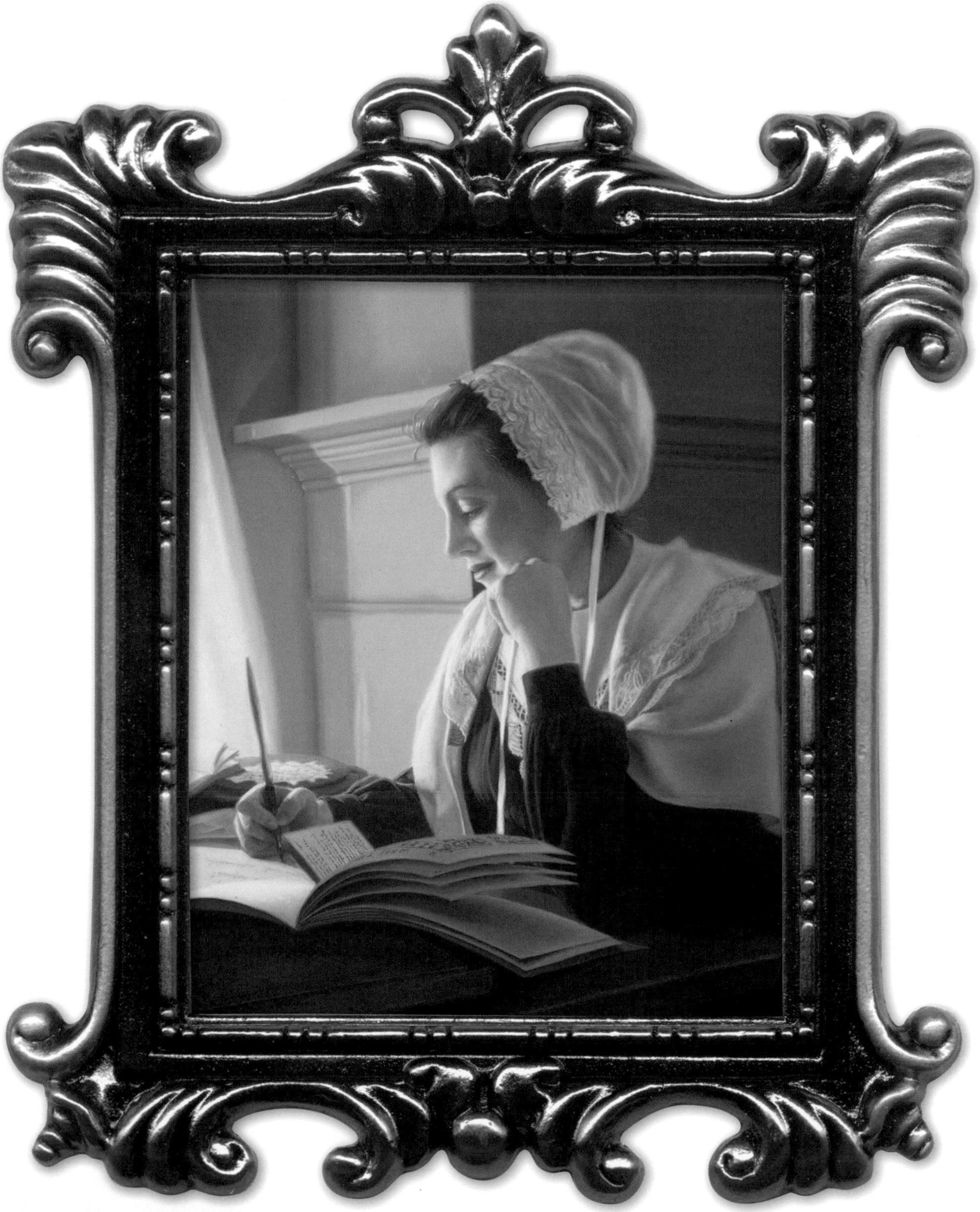

SORROW and SEPARATION

For he shall lay his hands upon thee, and thou shalt receive
the Holy Ghost . . . And thou needest not fear . . .

—Revelation to Emma, Doctrine & Covenants 25:8–9

The Holy Ghost shall be thy constant companion . . .

—Revelation to Emma, Doctrine & Covenants 121:46

During the years of their marriage, Joseph was often away from Emma and his young family. As he preached to members, tried to earn sufficient money to end his and the Church's debt, appealed to the government for the restitution of the Saints' rights, suffered unlawful imprisonments, and hid from the enemies of the Church, his heart must have been torn between his love of the Church he so vigorously defended and the soul mate he so deeply cherished.

For Emma, Joseph's work meant lonely months struggling to raise her children on her own while facing alone the terrifying persecutions of the world. These forlorn, recurring months apart added sorely to a life marred by frequent poverty and the wrenching loss of many of their dear little ones. Joseph and Emma's marriage was blessed with eleven children, two of whom were adopted.

As she bravely endured being separated from her beloved, how her arms must have ached for the six of those infants who were lowered into cold, desolate graves.

It is clear, then, why the Lord felt to tell each of them in revelation that the Holy Ghost would be a companion to whom they could turn (see D&C 121 and 25). It is possible that the Lord's call to Emma to compile the hymnal for the Church was a blessing of comfort. Consider the words to "How Firm a Foundation," one of the songs she chose for the original hymnal: "When through the deep waters I call thee to go, The rivers of sorrow shall not thee o'erflow, For I will be with thee, thy troubles to bless, And sanctify to thee thy deepest distress."[1] This quenching promise was no doubt what Joseph and Emma clung to as they waited for each sweet reunion.

1. *Hymns*, no. 85

LETTER FROM EMMA TO JOSEPH

WRITTEN IN QUINCY, ILLINOIS ❦ 7 MARCH 1839

Written while Emma waited for Joseph to be freed from Liberty Jail.

I shall not attempt to write my feelings altogether for the situation in which you are—the walls, bars and bolts, rolling rivers, running streams, rising hills, sinking valleys and spreading prairies that separate us—and the cruel injustice that first cast you into prison and still holds you there.

LETTER FROM EMMA TO JOSEPH

WRITTEN IN UNKNOWN LOCATION ❦ APRIL 1837

Joseph is hiding at the time of this letter, sending correspondence to Emma from various locations so his enemies cannot find him.

I cannot tell you my feelings when I found I could not see you before you left, yet I expect you can realize them; the children feel very anxious about you because they don't know where you have gone.

LETTER FROM JOSEPH TO EMMA

WRITTEN IN NEW YORK CITY, NEW YORK ❦ 13 OCTOBER 1832

After beholding all that I had any desire to behold, I returned to my room to meditate and calm my mind, and behold, the thoughts of home, of Emma and Julia, rushes upon my mind like a flood, and I . . . wish for the moment to be with them. My breast is filled with all the feelings and tenderness of a parent and a husband; and could I be with you, I would tell you many things.

LETTER FROM JOSEPH TO EMMA

WRITTEN IN RICHMOND, MISSOURI ❦ SENT TO FAR WEST, MISSOURI
12 NOVEMBER 1838

Oh God, grant that I may have the privilege of seeing once more my lovely family in the enjoyment of the sweets of liberty and social life. To press them to my bosom and kiss their lovely cheeks would fill my heart with unspeakable gratitude. [Emma,] tell the children that I am alive and trust I shall come and see them before long. Comfort their hearts all you can, and try to be comforted yourself, all you can.

CONSOLATION *in* COMPANIONSHIP

Thy friends do stand by thee, and they shall
hail thee again with warm hearts and friendly hands.

—Revelation to Joseph, Doctrine & Covenants 121:9

And the office of thy calling shall be for a comfort
unto . . . thy husband, in his afflictions.

—Revelation to Emma, Doctrine & Covenants 25:5

After receiving one of Emma's carefully penned missives, Joseph wrote, "I received your letter, which I read over and over again. It was a sweet morsel to me."[1] Those sentiments let us in on a loving companionship and depict the comfort Joseph and Emma provided each other—in letters when apart, and in a bond of close partnership when together. The couple was well-suited to each other in temperament, and both would be remembered for their jovial natures. Each had a quick wit, a gift that must have helped them survive the heartrending trials that characterized so much of their lives.

Emma found great pleasure in music, and as she worked at even mundane chores the notes of simple hymns floated on the air, coaxed into life by her untrained yet beautifully lilting soprano voice. The Lord Himself proclaimed that "the song of the righteous [was] a prayer" unto Him (D&C 25:12), and how Joseph's troubled heart must have been soothed by the comforting verses rendered in a voice he loved so well.

Indeed, the Lord specifically assigned Emma the calling of being a "comfort" to her husband (D&C 25:5). And in a companionship that knew not the limits of mortality, Joseph honored and sought to comfort Emma as much as she comforted him. Benjamin F. Johnson, Joseph's friend and secretary, once said of Joseph that "as a husband and father, his devotion to [family] stopped only at idolatry," and that his life's greatest motto after "God and His Kingdom" was that of "wives [and] children. . . ."[2]

1. Letter from Joseph Smith in Richmond, Missouri, to Emma Smith in Far West, Missouri, 12 November 1838. Cited in Jessee, Dean C., ed. *Personal Writings of Joseph Smith.* Provo, Brigham Young University Press, 1984, 405.

2. Andrus, Hyrum L., *Joseph Smith: The Man and the Seer; Tributes to the Prophet Joseph from Friend, Foe, & Acquaintances.* American Fork, Covenant Communications, 2005, 52.

LETTER FROM JOSEPH TO EMMA

WRITTEN IN NEW YORK CITY, NEW YORK ❦ 13 OCTOBER 1832

I feel as if I wanted to say something to you to comfort you in your peculiar trial and present affliction. I hope God will give you strength that you may not faint. I pray God to soften the hearts of those around you to be kind to you and take the burden off your shoulders as much as possible and not afflict you. I feel for you, for I know your state and that others do not, but you must comfort yourself knowing that God is your friend in heaven and that you have one true and living friend on earth, your husband.

LETTER FROM JOSEPH TO EMMA

WRITTEN IN LIBERTY JAIL, MISSOURI ❦ SENT TO QUINCY, ILLINOIS
21 MARCH 1839

My dear Emma, I very well know your toils and sympathize with you. If God will spare my life once more to have the privilege of taking care of you, I will ease your care and endeavor to comfort your heart.

PATRIARCHAL BLESSING
OF EMMA HALE SMITH

GIVEN BY JOSEPH SMITH SR. IN KIRTLAND, OHIO ❦ 9 DECEMBER 1834

[EMMA,] THY SOUL HAS BEEN AFFLICTED BECAUSE OF THE WICKEDNESS OF MEN IN SEEKING THE DESTRUCTION OF THY COMPANION, AND THY WHOLE SOUL HAS BEEN DRAWN OUT IN PRAYER FOR HIS DELIVERANCE; REJOICE, FOR THE LORD THY GOD HAS HEARD THY SUPPLICATIONS.

LETTER FROM EMMA TO JOSEPH

WRITTEN IN QUINCY, ILLINOIS ❦ MARCH 1839

I am . . . willing to suffer more if it is the will of kind heaven that I should for your sake. . . . I hope there are better days to come to us yet. . . . I am ever yours affectionately.

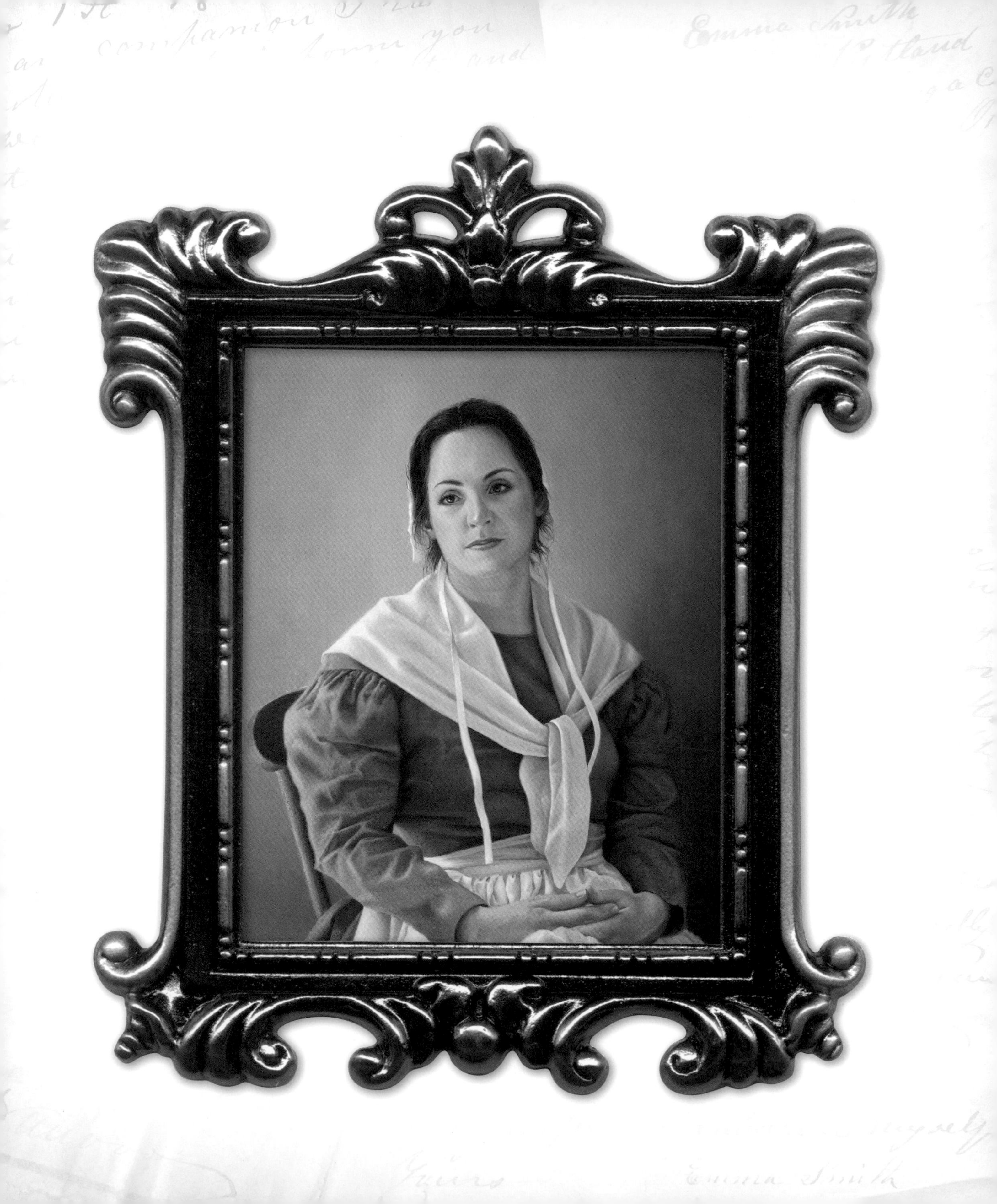
companion
Emma Smith
Emma Smith

FAITH *in* ADVERSITY

Wherefore, lift up thy heart and rejoice,
and cleave unto the covenants which thou hast made.

—Revelation to Emma, Doctrine & Covenants 25:13

Thine adversity and thine afflictions shall be but a small moment;
And then, if thou endure it well, God shall exalt thee on high.

—Revelation to Joseph, Doctrine & Covenants 121:7–8

Joseph once declared, "If I were sunk into the lowest pit . . . and all the Rocky Mountains piled on top of me, I ought not to be discouraged, but hang on, exercise faith, and keep up good courage, and I should come out on the top of the heap."[1]

What was the source of such stalwart faith? A merciful Father cradled both Emma and Joseph in His hands as they developed faith in the same way all of us must—line upon line, precept upon precept. That faith was bolstered as Joseph tenderly placed each infant in a freshly dug grave; as Emma worked to carefully pick the tar from Joseph's blistered skin; as Joseph and Emma clung desperately to each other in a tearful embrace the morning he set out for Carthage.

Joseph was not impervious to frustration and impatience. Cried he from the filthy confines of Liberty Jail, "O God, where art thou?" (D&C 121:1). The pain evident in that cry reveals a student still learning from the Master Teacher. Indeed, in response, the Lord not only comforts Joseph but also gently teaches, reminding Joseph to put his trials in perspective as he developed more patience and faith. His divine tutorial also extended to Emma, who was reminded, "Murmur not because of the things which thou hast not seen," and who was told to "seek for the things of a better [world]" (D&C 25: 4, 10).

The Lord, who sees all things from the beginning to the end, knew with a perfect knowledge that if Joseph and Emma would "lift up [their] heart[s] and rejoice, and cleave unto the covenants" they had made, they would make it through (see D&C 25:13). In a determination to put His promise to the test, both Emma and Joseph mustered the strength to persevere, making theirs a journey filled with the faith to overcome.

1. Jarvis, Zora Smith, comp. *George A. Smith Family.* Provo, Brigham Young University Press, 1962, 54.

LETTER FROM EMMA TO JOSEPH

WRITTEN IN QUINCY, ILLINOIS ❦ 21 MARCH 1839

Was it not for conscious innocence and the direct interposition of divine mercy, I am very sure I never should have been able to have endured the scenes of suffering that I have passed through . . . but I still live and am yet willing to suffer more.

LETTER FROM EMMA TO HER SON, JOSEPH SMITH III

1869

I have seen many, yes very many, trying scenes in my life in which I could not see . . . where any good could come of them. . . . But yet I feel a divine trust in God that all things shall work for good.

ABOUT EMMA

WRITTEN BY LUCY MACK SMITH IN
The History of Joseph Smith by His Mother

I HAVE NEVER SEEN A WOMAN IN MY LIFE WHO WOULD ENDURE EVERY SPECIES OF FATIGUE AND HARDSHIP, FROM MONTH TO MONTH, AND FROM YEAR TO YEAR, WITH THAT UNFLINCHING COURAGE, ZEAL AND PATIENCE WHICH [EMMA] HAS EVER DONE. . . . IT MAY BE THAT MANY MAY HAVE TO ENCOUNTER THE SAME. . . . MAY THEY HAVE GRACE GIVEN THEM ACCORDING TO THEIR DAY, EVEN AS HAS BEEN THE CASE WITH HER.

LETTER FROM JOSEPH TO EMMA

WRITTEN IN GREENVILLE, INDIANA
SENT TO KIRTLAND, OHIO
6 JUNE 1832

I will try to be contented with my lot knowing that God is my friend. In him I shall find comfort. I have given my life into his hands. I am prepared to go at his call. I desire to be with Christ. I count not my life dear to me, only to do his will.

LETTER FROM JOSEPH TO EMMA

WRITTEN IN INDEPENDENCE, MISSOURI ♥ SENT TO FAR WEST, MISSOURI
4 NOVEMBER 1838

What God may do for us I do not know, but I hope for the best always in all circumstances. Although I go unto death, I will trust in God.

REUNION and PEACE

My son, peace be unto thy soul. . . .
And the doctrine of the priesthood shall distil upon thy soul as the dews from heaven.

—Revelation to Joseph, Doctrine & Covenants 121: 7, 45

My daughter. . . . Verily I say unto thee that thou shalt lay aside
the things of this world, and seek for the things of a better.

—Revelation to Emma, Doctrine & Covenants 25: 1, 10

As Joseph left for Carthage, Emma—surely knowing in her sorrowing heart what was ahead—requested a blessing. Not having time, the Prophet told her to write the best blessing she could, and he would sign it when he returned. Seeking the Spirit as she wrote, Emma penned the blessing. Joseph never returned.

Widowed in her late thirties, Emma was still a young mother when the mobs cut down her beloved Joseph; her last child was born just months after his death. Despite her anguish and the tragedies she endured, she lived nearly thirty-five years after tenderly preparing his body for burial. "Ever his affectionately," Emma's mind must have often lingered on the restored keys allowing the eternal sealing of families—the crowning gift among the doctrines of the priesthood—and the comfort inherent in that promise.

As Emma's final days drew near, she reported a vision in which Joseph came to her. In the dream she put on her bonnet and shawl and went with him: "I did not think that it was anything unusual. I went with him into a [beautiful] mansion, and he showed me through the different apartments." One room was a nursery, and there she saw with joy an infant in the cradle. Emma continued, "I knew my babe, my Don Carlos that was taken from me."

Emma sprang forward, caught the child up in her arms, held him to her exultant heart, and wept with joy. Recovered from the overwhelming emotion of once again holding her little one, she turned to Joseph and asked, "Joseph, where are the rest of my children?" He responded, "Emma, be patient and you shall have all your children."

As her vision closed, Emma saw standing by Joseph's side a personage of light, even the Lord Jesus Christ.[1] That vision must have been a final seal of peace upon Emma's heart, writing upon it her precious sealing to Joseph on that beautiful spring day in 1843.

A few days later, Emma trembled at the threshold of eternity, surrounded by her loved ones. Suddenly she raised herself up, stretched out her hand, and called, "Joseph! Joseph!" Then, sinking back against her son's arm, she clasped her hands on her chest and was gone.[2] At last they were together once more—Joseph and Emma, hearts twined as one, never to be separated again.

1. Gracia N. Jones, *Emma and Lucy,* American Fork, Covenant Communications, 2005, 190.
2. Ibid.

LETTER FROM JOSEPH TO EMMA

WRITTEN IN INDEPENDENCE, MISSOURI ❦ SENT TO FAR WEST, MISSOURI

4 NOVEMBER 1838

Oh Emma, do not forsake me nor the truth, but remember if I do not meet you again in this life, may God grant that we may meet in heaven. I cannot express my feelings—my heart is full. Farewell, oh my kind and affectionate Emma. I am forever your husband and true friend.

WRITTEN BY JOSEPH ABOUT EMMA

1842

Referring to the events of August 1842 when he was in hiding and Emma participated in subterfuge to be able to see him.

What unspeakable delight and what transports of joy swelled my bosom when I took by the hand . . . my beloved Emma—she that was my wife, even the wife of my youth, and the choice of my heart. Many were the reverberations of my mind when I contemplated for a moment the many scenes we had been called to pass through, the fatigues and the toils, the sorrows and sufferings, and joys and consolations, from time to time, which had strewed our path and crowned our board. Oh what a commingling of thought filled my mind for the moment, again she is here, even in the seventh trouble—undaunted, firm, and unwavering—unchangeable, affectionate Emma!

PATRIARCHAL BLESSING
OF EMMA HALE SMITH

GIVEN BY JOSEPH SMITH SR. IN KIRTLAND, OHIO ☙ 9 DECEMBER 1834

THOU SHALT SEE MANY DAYS, YEA, THE LORD
WILL SPARE THEE TILL THOU ART SATISFIED.
FOR THOU SHALT SEE THY REDEEMER.
THY HEART SHALL REJOICE IN THE GREAT
WORK OF THE LORD, AND NO ONE SHALL
TAKE THY REJOICING FROM THEE.

EMMA . . . THOU ART BLESSED OF THE
LORD, FOR THY FAITHFULNESS AND TRUTH,
THOU SHALT BE BLESSED WITH THY HUSBAND,
AND REJOICE IN THE GLORY WHICH SHALL
COME UPON HIM.

right to take either
or the printing office
the same since
person but Wm
your delivering either
my husband or the
person, untill further
further, we have been
individuals, that
Post Office are permitted
seen examining, over-
letters and papers
and reading the
law and your
upon you
necessary
at large
private interests
With sentiments of
Yours
Emma Smith